NOW THAT'S BIG

SUEZ

Published by Creative Education
P.O. Box 227, Mankato, Minnesota 56002
Creative Education is an imprint of The Creative Company
www.thecreativecompany.us

Design and Production by The Design Lab
Printed in the United States of America

Photographs by Alamy (2d Alan King, Joe Baraban, BennettPhoto, Ian M
Butterfield, James Davis Photography, Mary Evans Picture Library, Profimedia
International s.r.o., Robert Harding Picture Library Ltd., SCPhotos)

Library of Congress Cataloging-in-Publication Data
Riggs, Kate.
Suez Canal / by Kate Riggs.
p. cm. — (Now that's big!)
Includes index.
ISBN 978-1-58341-706-5
1. Suez Canal (Egypt)—Juvenile literature. I. Title. II. Series.
HE543.R54 2009   386'.43—dc22   2007052342

First edition

9 8 7 6 5 4 3 2 1

CREATIVE EDUCATION

C A N A L

BY KATE RIGGS

The Suez (*SOO-ehz*) Canal is a waterway. It is in a country called Egypt. It connects two different seas that have land between them. It lets ships get through the hot, dry desert.

Sailing around the tip of Africa was often dangerous

6

A man from France
named Ferdinand de
Lesseps wanted to build
the canal. He thought
it would help ships save a lot of time.
The ships would not have to sail
around Africa. They could go through
it instead.

When the canal was finished, many people celebrated

8

De Lesseps hired Egyptian people to dig the Suez Canal. They started working on it in 1859. They used their bare hands, shovels, and baskets to dig. Later on, de Lesseps got machines for them to use.

1859

Camels could not cross the canal without boarding a ship

Camels are animals that live in deserts. Like ships, they are also used to carry people and goods.

It took 10 years to dig the Suez Canal. About 2.4 million Egyptians worked on it. They made it 100 miles (160 km) long and 175 feet (53 m) wide.

1869

Huge ships that carry oil often travel through the canal

12

Lots of water plants and fish live in the Suez Canal. Some crabs live there, too.

The land the Suez Canal passes through is flat. Ships can just float on the water from one end of the canal to the other.

The Suez Canal is deep enough for most ships to travel on. But some ships are too big.

Lots of people and goods travel on the Suez Canal. It had to be made bigger so that more ships could use it. Today, it is 120 miles (192 km) long.

People in small boats sell goods in cities like Ismailia

Ismailia (iz-MALE-ee-ah) is a beautiful city. It is along the edge of the Suez Canal.

16

More than 15,000 ships travel through the Suez Canal every year. Ships carry oil, coal, grains, and metals. It takes a ship about 14 hours to get all the way through the canal.

Riding a ferry is an easy way to get from place to place

18

Big boats called ferries take people through the Suez Canal.

People who visit the Suez Canal can ride on a boat. Or they can drive on the road that is next to the canal. The best time of year to visit the canal is between December and March. The desert is not so hot then.

For almost 150 years, the canal has been a major waterway

The Suez Canal is a big help to people in Egypt. Whenever people use it, they are thankful for their special shortcut through the desert.

The city of Port Said (sy-EED) is at the entrance *of the Suez Canal. It is a busy place.*

GLOSSARY

Africa—*one of Earth's seven large pieces of land*

desert—*a place that is dry because it does not get much rain*

entrance—*an opening or beginning place*

goods—*things that people sell to make money*

READ MORE ABOUT IT

Landau, Elaine. *Canals.* New York: Children's Press/Scholastic, 2000.

Gibbons, Gail. *Mummies, Pyramids, and Pharaohs: A Book about Ancient Egypt.* New York: Little, Brown Books for Young Readers, 2004.

24

INDEX